Copyright ©2016 by Tina Thurston
Revised edition 2019

All rights reserved. No portion of this book may be reproduced in any manner whatsoever without written permission except in the case of brief quotations embodied in critical articles and reviews.

Author website: www.tinathurston.com

Cover art by: Sanne Aßmann
ISBN: 978-0-9863623-5-4

Other publications by Tina Thurston:
"Rose Marie Lynn and her Fallen Feline Friend"
(this is an illustrated children's book written with foster children ages 7-9 in mind, and for anyone young at heart).

Connected to source, a journey of experience.

POEMS

by
Tina Thurston

preface

Writing poetry began in my teen years. The rhymes flowed spontaneously while journaling. Journaling was first by school assignment in my teenage years which transitioned into a habit in adulthood.

I believe in the power of thoughts, they manifest experience. I believe in the power of words written. For me, words written no longer compete for space within my thoughts.

I was not aware of the self healing process through journaling until my mid-twenties. I was in therapy and was told I didn't need to be there as I had already figured out the best therapy for me.

I was told to never stop writing.

In the three years since the first publication of this book there has been the opportunity for greater reflection and personal growth.

Rather than give power to the abuse that occured in my childhood by documenting it here as I did in the first edition, I would like to simply state "to forgive is to move forward consciously and continuosly."

As we walk our path of healing from whatever trauma's are experienced, please find a support system and know you are not alone. Know there are many resources available to assist in your growth to peace within. You are worthy. You are loved.

I am grateful to have the ability to create relatable art that gives thought to the emotional aspects of the human experience.

Let the poems tell the story. A journey of experience.

contents

1	conquer
2	observer
3	redemption
4	believe
5	vapid
6	see
7	alone
8	grow
9	focus
10	tricky
11	multidimensional
12,13	love
14	transformation
15	misadventures
16	quest
17	ashes
18	change
19	spin
20,21	momentary
22,23	journey
24	prepares
25	debt
26,27	hell
28	somewhere
29	music
30	find
31	build
32	learning
33	circle
34,35	clarity
36	cycles
37	reason
38	aligns
39	forgotten
40	contract
41	relate
42	learned
43	hope
44,45	voice
46	feeling
47	giving
48,49	remembrance

50	time
51	illusion
52	gently
53	goddess
54	becoming
55	truth
56	accept
57	trying
58,59	retreat
60	someone
61	growing
62,63	wonderment
64	poet
65	wish
66	leeches
67	actions
68	blessings
69	anticipation
70	release
71	commitment
72	pretend
73	boys
74	checkmate
75	found
76	true
77	birth
78	bond
79	formation
80	glance
81	angel
82	smitten
83	addicted
84	unopened
85	expansion
86	memories
87	partner
88	mountain
89	stillness
90	awakened

Connected to source,
a journey of experience.

conquer

Why do I have to be here?
I really don't know.
I try so hard to please them
but I guess it doesn't show.
Everything has to be so hard for me
I wish I could know why.
Did I really agree to this before I came here,
to suffer all my life?
I wish I had my mother
so I could tell her how I feel,
but I know my thoughts to her, really don't appeal.
She left me when I was young
to make it on my own.
Oh, how I want to see her today
so she can see how I've grown.
I wish I had a family so that I could have some love
but everyone just tells me to look to my father above.
Am I going crazy because I don't know the way?
I am left to CONQUER this life by living it day to day.

*written at 17 years old. My first poem.

observer

Keep your eyes open
life's a calculated move.
Backseat is the OBSERVER,
front seat molds to you.
A calm resides in knowing nothing more to say.
Time gives the hardest lessons,
filters out those who stay.
Catch the wind riding on a silk thread.
May we collide in space,
passing through then back again,
a vaguely familiar face.
A sensation comes alive in memory of you.
Nothing passes but what we call time,
in a humans linear view.
Remain the observer unemotionally driven.
To those true to themselves,
the greatest gift is given.

redemption

...and when the friend returns, I ask-
Which door is mine to walk through?
-the one slightly cracked enough to see faint light?
-the one darker inside than where I now stand?
-the one that smells of falling rain to keep me in a state of slumber?
-the one illuminated brightly which makes me wonder...
Which door would be the threshold as the answer changes day to day?
Each decision made forges a new direction to take.
-it would be the door slightly ajar
A step inside reveals the path afar.
The longest path is the friend who calls
and walks beside or not at all.
The longest path as I look back
the door has not changed its position.
I could stop and turn back,
this is not the answer for REDEMPTION.
stand still
There is movement in separation.
Grounded down in a place of preparation.
The longest path ahead.
The beckoning door behind.
Answers lay dormant in the pathways of the mind.
be still
be still

believe

I wish I could be the 'pretty in pink' girl.
I wish I were funded by daddy's bank roll world.
I wish for some relief from this life full of pain.
I wish to talk to something outside of my brain.
My external chattering seems to fall on deaf ears,
nothing but the same ol' days left in here.
I sit, I write, I hope, I pray,
for some kind of miracle to be ushered this way.
Some kind of force field passing over my space,
to get me up out of this recycled place.
Make me BELIEVE all my life has a purpose
to open my eyes wider to an untarnished surface.
I sit, I pace, and contemplate,
the unseen forces swirling to decide and provide my fate.

vapid

Such a beautiful corpse you make,
skin so flawless it appears plastic and fake.
I ever so gently push back your hair
to get a better view of your VAPID stare.
I lean in close to give a tender kiss
only 3 minutes ago, your breath I missed.
Don't worry my love, at least you 'died pretty'
with a heart as cold and calloused as any major U.S. city.
Your surgically enhanced chest will never rise with another breath.
Your impossibly long fingers will never hold another's hand.
It's probable your spirit is hovering nearby
wishing you had made me your final man.
It's too late to think about what could have become.
It was a beautiful sight as you struggled for the gun.
You never wanted to grow old, shriveled and wrinkled anyway.
I did you the kindest favor releasing this body of yours
under my devotion and care you will stay.

see

You say I SEE the world through rose colored glasses?
perhaps, I should look at it through green

Green for all the jealousy that occurs
when people are envious of another's accomplishments

Or maybe red…yeah red…to see all the anger people have
and express and hurt others with

Or maybe black…black so I can hide behind this color
and choose not to see at all

No, I think i'd like yellow…yellow to amplify
the suns rays on the beauty that nature provides

Or… maybe rose
I think rose is a nice color

Rose…like a child with rosy cheeks from the cool breath of winter
or a baby with rosy cheeks who's just awakened from a long nap

Rose…rose is a nice color, it's simple
and a rose is a most beautiful thing on this earth to see

So, why do you not look through rose colored glasses?
Could it be you're afraid to see the beauty of your world?

alone

Time passes,
why does not the memories of my mind pass?
Rivers flow, they have somewhere to go.
If changes are constant, why are things the same?
I feel pain, I hurt.
People come into my mind- they laugh, they ridicule, but mostly they leave me ALONE.
Footprints in snow eventually fade away.
Time passes slowly yet fast.
The years of life are gone, mountains stay.
Oceans drift and flow soothing me to sleep.
Time passes.

grow

I don't know why I am the way I am
I don't know why I do the things I do
I don't have parents to emulate, like most of you
I go with my thoughts and how I feel
often wondering what is real
It seems so often to me, my thoughts stray far from reality
somewhere out there stuck in a dream
out where there is no need to scream
out where love rules everything
somewhere life's losers are, with no need to take blame
They have a place where they can go
a place where they can actually GROW
grow up to develop into all they can be
without the need to escape reality
They can fall asleep anytime they need
to rest their eyes, their souls, in a dream
Am I to build this place?
I wonder
I wonder where my life goes now
I know its changing but not sure how
I want to be happy, productive, and useful
I want to play, be o.k. , with my heart and soul full

focus

I catch my sleep here and there
rhyming in tongues of "I don't care!"
each person inside
scared to be
to show
or be labeled insane
I don't know
but
I do love them all
I embrace them in fact
I feel their emotions and thoughts are intact
FOCUS together
together we stay
focused on believing
for a much better day

tricky

Straight up from the gutter and like no other
tried your neighborhood on for size
but it gave way too many lies.
Tried to fit a zig zag into a straight and proper line.
Umbrella of judgment and oppression
killed my soul time after time.
now...
It's time I revisited my childhood as I turn the bad stuff into good.
You can't ignore where you came from
it's what made you who you are now.
Remembrance yet forgetting, is the TRICKY tightrope walked somehow.

multidimensional

So many people are inside of me
it's sometimes hard to figure out which one I should be.
Shattered personality or
MULTIDIMENSIONAL
my purse is empty but my heart is full.
Society would have me locked away,
locked away if they knew I wrote this way.
Oh, it's because of her childhood they'd say
fuck that! I am who I am today!
I have lived, I survive.
I survive to write so that others know,
all the emotions a soul can show
all the beauty that you can see
flowing in and out of me
all the rage and hatred to
feeling and showing
it's nothing new.

love

I like my imperfections
they remind me I am alive.
I was once a broke down stripper
and that is not a lie.
I was once a wife who lived in suburbia
it gave me nothing close to sanity
but I've heard of ya...
The only thing that still remains
is I'm a mother in my blood.
I've given birth to two human beings
and cared for them as I could.
This life so far has taught me
to be stronger than I thought I could be.
It ain't so easy growing up wrong
without a mom or daddy.
It ain't so easy to be a number in a system
to be a foster kid shuttled through.
It taught me early to grow up fast
and to have faith in something to.
There were sorrows I once cried for.
Too many men saw me as their silent whore
but...
who I am deep down inside
is a mystery to most, my thoughts I hide.
I expose enough to relate somehow
when this life is over
will I take a bow?
or...

Will I silently exit as though I never existed?
A life lived ordinary under false pretenses.
A life lived in a series of stories,
to the children I loved
mom didn't reach her glory
but, she did leave you
in a better place for care
cause on this planet
we're all too aware
that it takes having money
to do more than just get by
it takes being tough
and sometimes a good cry
but make no mistake
for all I've done and feel
my LOVE for those who are dear to me
is all that was ever real.

transformation

Strap on the heels its time to do a show.
Slide the skirt up past my thighs some have come to know.
Place the bra on just right
as soul and body prepare to take flight.
Leaving this physical plane for a small moment in time,
wings of angels congregate to lend me this rhyme.
Twist and move with the subtlety of power,
body parts do mesmerize and make lesser men cower.
Time to become what others see in me,
all the parts of a diamond shining bright,
falling leaves from my tree.
TRANSFORMATION takes its toll
sleepless nights I've come to know.
Dreams are a dream and have eluded me,
so here I dance in reality.

misadventures

Why do I feel it necessary to revisit these places?
Painful thoughts, tarnished past,
half smiles on some faces.
Feel a space so commonplace
importance of my looks don't matter.
Respect is given on my hard knock life
not useless educated chatter.
Born into it this way
my mom was just a showgirl;
probably the kind on the most bottom rung
in the hierarchy of beautiful power.
I've tasted that life of power and beauty,
of bumper car love
that becomes so fleeting.
You're here, and now you're gone
your light comes and goes
some hearts are won.
Slow rhythm of one's body
head held high in the night.
Touch me only if granted permission.
The bum outside lives a life of fright.
Lying alone on the sidewalk
we pass him by to catch our ride.
Another night come.
Another night gone.
MISADVENTURES of a searching soul
combined with others
we are one.

quest

How much of life is living just under the radar?
Push the envelope a little bit, take the common mind too far.
Pull back and stay under
observe the worker ants as they scatter.
Fill your bubble of love and light
duality of nature, conformity of an image.
Love and hate become the same
complacency fuels a self rage.

I will not settle for the common view
too much to see before this life is through.
A rest cycle is much in need,
on the never ending QUEST, life breeds a greed.
It could go both ways, lonely days spent in a haze,
or floating above this world.
An inner child awaits to play
something more than just a girl.

ashes

Toss a lit match on the bed to watch it burn.
Sacred turntable became a sealed urn
full of ashes & essence of a mortal once present.
The burn will change.
The pain is the same.
Can the fire be so wrong for being a fire?
Caverned chest becomes hollowed.
A recycled pill one cannot swallow,
to make a glue that binds within...
From in the fetal to feet underneath
a shaky step generations bequeath.
Is the bed still burning?
Is a head still churning out prisons in visions & dreams?
A prison of flesh makes a soul act reckless.
When all one wants is to watch the past burn,
to rise from the ASHES and be freed from the urn.

change

What is it with all these memories?
they're all just moments in time
pictures and places
love painted faces
wandering round in my mind

people that love
Angels sent from above
Demons from hell
faces CHANGE where they dwell

from earth to life
they stay alive, they drift
never giving me my peace

I'm tired I say
just go away
leave my mind
so I can sleep

these are all just moments in time
suspended yet long lived
my heart and soul forever entwined
with all the shit life gives

spin

Don't fight it
ignite it
watch it burn bright
brighter than white
cuts through the night
flies through the darkness
the evil, the doom
even the shadows that like to loom
loom about watching
watching me watching you
turn on your light
don't be afraid
don't fear what you don't see
if you don't give yourself a chance
you might never learn to dance
dance away the anger
throw your arms at the invisible pain
SPIN yourself
kick the air
let it out
then lay down
let the tears flow
fall from your eyes
like rain
rain that flows
making rivers and oceans
back and forth
like human emotions

momentary

Just for today,
I must put my imagination to rest,
the whirlwind of thoughts and mental chatter
have caused me much distress.
Why can't I be one of those,
with vacant eyes and joyful prose?
For a girl to grow up in this world
without a mom or a dad
or her own place...
is where, 'Life's a bitch' came from.
It's why someone coined that phrase.
The only thing that mattered, I left so far behind...
all to go blindly forward
somewhere...
to lend my heart in rhyme.
-many bridges, some I've crossed
-many paths have made me lost
Lost on this earth, where I chose to be birthed.
Why? I still ask
right now in this moment
this earth can "kiss my ass"

Why do people say words that crumble fast as dirt?
-say the words of ones fake heart, where relationships start
-say the thoughts of ones mind, are sometimes kind
but, most words seem to be said for ones MOMENTARY
gain
as the world turns
as clouds drift by
where we are
remains the same
nothing changes except
the sun's position
a once offered loving arm
retreats in submission.

journey

It all started on a road that was paved with good intentions
the path was unmarked and never was mentioned...
the faces of loved ones left far behind
while the wheel of life turned, caught up in the grind
many windows are looked out of, the scenery has changed
the actors are different, the lessons the same
stillness and solitude are the comforts of grace
a souls wisest ambition has come to this place
a JOURNEY like no other
a quiet calm rests deep inside
children's laughter has silenced in this place I now hide
should love equal loss?
should fame equal glory?
what should be the price for a soul's pain filled story?
should the degree of sadness also be the degree of joy?
should it really matter if girls love girls and boys love boys?
What do I know?
there is a path for everyone
cast by moonlight
met by the sun

there is an evolution
of birth and death
where peace becomes found
as pain lays to rest

prepares

The path to oneself is a lonely road to take
filled with leeches and takers that only give heartbreak.
Yet somehow there's a way that is strewn with littered glass;
broken pieces are illuminated by the bright light of the sun,
while hateful words become corroded and crass.
A bird spreads her wings and PREPARES to take flight
to troubles and sorrows she wishes goodnight.
Love comes in false disguises
ice cold is a blanket of snow
hearts beat fast as temperature rises
false hope she swiftly comes to know.
The journey of intuition gives thoughts of souls a listen.
A life cycle comes full circle
a lesson completes again.
Through trials, accusations, and firm resolve
the completion of this life is gained.

debt

How can we ignore the violent destruction of people torn then resurrected?
Of violated houses in fear people stay, not having the power to go away.
They stay and they cry while their blood ties die.
Why all the violence, what does it get?
…more land to destroy
…more people in debt
Debt to hard labor they spend their days.
Whatever DEBT is unfinished their children will pay.

hell

Come little child and walk with me through the paths of this hellish land.
I'll only ignore your merciful plea's so come child take my hand.
See blood bathed streets of those who lay torn, those that gave so you would be born.
Oh little child are you listening, to the voices of strangers calling to thee?

Do you sense the harshness in the groans surrounding their words?
Their lustful imagination will destroy young flesh and blood.
They will say they love and want you, you can have from them anything,
but in time you see, they will leave you, to blindly find your own way.

These visions I know are sure to haunt you, through the years of your life to come.
Don't you know child to trust in me? I am the Holy one
These souls on the streets are old and demented, don't succumb to them at all,
for if you stray to their wishes and needs your soul is bound to fall.

I told you that you can trust in me, I won't ever let you down.

Why is it child you are gazing at me with that foolish questioning frown?

No child I will not leave you, but what are you thinking of now?
You say you have desire to kill me, for leading you to this town.

Well let me tell you something child you should never have trusted in me,
because now I have captured your young naive soul to be tortured endlessly.

Yes, my child, you see that I...am just like all of these poor souls,
the ones I warned you to refrain from, now the truth is told.

Goodbye child, oh! but there is one more fact to tell,
after the years of your life are past I will surely greet you in HELL!

(written at 17 years old)

somewhere

Is there SOMEWHERE a life less wasted,
a love thats tasted and built upon?
Is there somewhere a soul matching faces,
of patterns and places we've dreamed upon?
Is there somewhere a kindness unmeasured,
by the cost of ones treasures, or the price of your clothes?
Is there somewhere a love waiting for me, completing the story?
I'd like to know.

music

Did i say something that wasn't right?
Did we part forever without a fight?
Your life is set and mine never was,
been drifting since birth into an abyss of drugless justice.
Music is my drug.
Music heals my soul.
It calms me in my headspace
where nature makes me whole.
Music doesn't ask me questions and it doesn't tell me lies,
it comforts me in times of need, withholds its alibis.
Its been holding me together since I can remember,
runs through my thickening blood.
Uplifts me forever, music is my drug...
and
MUSIC is my home.
Though my body is everywhere and nowhere
my soul continues to roam.
Poker face becomes displaced, eyes penetrate the unknown.
The wall is higher than ever before, forever,
music is my home.

<u>find</u>

It must feel cold to have no soul
your purpose in the world unseen,
existing day to day in the usual way society tells you to be.
Break away from the mold before you're too old,
live the way your heart guides you
no matter what people say.
You've got to FIND your own way within the inner light provided you.
It's in your heart, your soul, your mind,
it's how you treat others to always be kind.
This life is hard I know.
I've been around and it shows.
Even the oldest of spirits are tried, when is it understood?
We're all just souls inhabiting bodies, trying our best to be good.

build

Again, I open my heart and it gets torn apart.
A laugh that is shared goes nowhere.
A love that is taken, a soul forsaken.
A heart unopened, a room left barren.
A soul left empty.
I am going to step away now and pretend I never fucking existed.
In my time line on this earth, life became so twisted.
All I wanted was to love someone and BUILD a home to rest,
but with everyone I open myself up to my sanity becomes a test.
I am a poet, a mother, and have even been called a saint.
My crying unheard, I bear my pain.
I share this pain and whore it for all to see because
when this life is done in the end my friend,
what is left? ...me

__learning__

I used to be an open book but in this world
conditions demand a second look.
I used to lay my heart out for all to see
but now it beats stronger inside of me.
I used to share my smile with all who passed by
but too many times the trolls made me cry.
The walking dead souls that come to play with my mind,
testing my patience and ability to be kind.
It's o.k. and it's alright,
I understand it's life's bitter plight.
I'm not coming back to this planet again,
learned my lessons,
my souls on the mend.
I am LEARNING patience, forgiveness,
and to love without fear.
I live somewhat detached,
though my presence is here.
We're all kind of climbing up our own self made hills.
We sometimes drown our pain with alcohol and colorful pills.
We can also simply choose to feel all that life has to give.
When this choice is understood,
it's then you begin to live.

circle

This world makes you tough and this world makes you wise,
as the blindfold unravels from innocent eyes.
A thread is sent forth attached to a star,
some come up close, others watch from afar.
A CIRCLE
A cycle of familiar faces,
reminders of the past seen in different places.
Circular and cellular, blood stirs a desire.
Human ambitions in overdrive, the aura spirals higher.
Consummate explosion, innocence is no longer.
Spiritual essence we become yet human form is stronger.

clarity

Glimpses of CLARITY stay close to my heart.
The way to serenity is to stay close to my heart,
while I take back my power I had at the start.
I breathe in the air that surrounds my soul,
comes to clean me and make me whole.
I'm calm in nature the place I find peace.
I touch the ground for souls release.
Whatever happens as each day unfolds,
I know
I know
nature holds my soul.
Ashes to ashes dust to dust,
it's few that walk this earth besides myself that I trust.
It is said 'the eyes are the window to the soul'
as we move and drift and come to know:
those we incarnate with life after life
who appear sometimes as mother, brother, or wife.
If you rise up above the pain that's so real,
a peace in your soul you will come to feel.
Rise up above it and view detached down below.
The earth keeps on turning as it carries these souls.

Expand your mind and open your heart.
Love one another as we loved at the start.
At the start of life's cycle we were full of love and life,
then lessons came along pressing imprints of strife.
we walk
we meet
we part
and meet again

cycles

A cloud of pessimism came above my head
filtered into my heart and claimed my bed.
Suddenly life became heavy and thick.
I tried to fly but the fog did its trick.
Exchange of clouded eyes and mouth full of lies
the game is on again.
Detachment reigns to numb the pain,
creation dies within.
A time to live a time to die,
CYCLES repeated without a try.
Cease to swallow the syrup of sludge,
reconstitute life from a friends gentle nudge.
Re-spark the kindle that propels forward movement,
my body lies dormant minds eye incongruent.
An understanding of fluidity of flow
come to know, cycles.

reason

Once again,
the warmth of my tears feel good on my skin.
Once again, crying to relieve life's frustrations.
I wish I could forgive without hesitation.
I wish I could be at a place in life
where I stand high on my mountain
and feel no strife.
I wish I could be in a place of no sorrow
where today has created a better tomorrow.
I write these words yet,
I'm done with words said to me.
Without action or respect, leave me be.
There must be a REASON I am this way,
full of sadness inside that's rooted to stay.
words are written
words erased
no definition
on anyone's face
alone again with my own water as my friend
at least my tears I know
stay with me until the end…

aligns

It's a permeating sadness I just cant seem to shake.
For everything I give this world,
it delights in more to take.
For every elevation reached,
for every false contract signed and breached
this world, it tires me down.
Holding me down to remind me of
what it wants me to be.
Seldom a shot of a second time around.
Stay right there where you should be.
Stay in the line you were born.
Don't rise too high or we'll remind you,
in half you're torn.
Once in awhile a human appears to remind me-
there is still good.
Once in awhile a message is sent to remind me-
rise up from being misunderstood.
Once in awhile words are shared to remind me-
there is a spiritual nature that cares.
Once in awhile, yes once in awhile
life ALIGNS and I don't feel so alone out here.

forgotten

Opened eyes were not so wise,
to trust again she met demise.
Falsely mislead the voices instead, directed her to the edge
where she stood.
Umbilicus ripped she lost her grip
on anything,
and everyone she knew.
Casing stripped she handled it, the other side may now have
won.
For its a dark place where light does fear
its a common place she lingers near,
for all FORGOTTEN without a face
she kneels once more in this sordid place.
To choose her battles, her justly cause
Angels & Demons both applause.
She's seen them both through veils of smoke,
through eyes so wise her own demise.

contract

If time is an illusion then why so much confusion
should look at the bigger picture,
instead of what's right here.
Rise above this planet earth,
hover and ponder your own birth.
Did you CONTRACT to come here and take from others?
or...
Did you contract to come here to love one another?
Power, Greed, Money, War!
What do these matter?
What's it all for?
If you were to stand alone with all you own on your shell;
would you still spew your greed and condemn others to hell?
Hold yourself up and remember your wings.
There are much more important parts to life than just 'things'.

relate

Peel back the layers and peer inside
no need to hide it's all in my eyes.
Any story that's inside to tell
has a layer of sweet icing to my personal hell.
It has been said that 'all pain is self chosen'
I'm quite sure I wasn't born to be this broken.
Those I RELATE to are few and far between.
I trod along a path mostly unseen and
retreat into nature where comfort is found.
Portions of mind remain in the happy place
while the physical body is bound.
I can relate to a panther pacing in it's cage:
-relate to the madman screaming in rage
-relate to the woman giving another its life
-relate to being a misunderstood wife.
As I continue to walk sometimes all alone,
sometimes with another, in pairs we roam.
So look in these eyes and continue to see
the multiple facets of a diamond to be.

learned

I'm tired of being the quiet, pretty face girl.
Dress me up and take me out but don't let me talk too much.
Look at me see what you see
now you look and don't touch.
Now you look at me from a distant place
once breathed my fire and kissed my face.
You wonder whatever made me turn.
What made me become bitter?
I LEARNED
I learned how to think this evil in the unholiest of life's
harshest lessons.
I learned how to defend my discolored honor with no need
for church bound confessions,
to a so called gods ordained priest.
I've made some peace to say the least.
I've expressed myself in low societies ways
and wondered how that ruined up my days.
but…
Now, I'm wiser and now I've learned.
No more getting faded, used up or burned.
I'm quiet within while my light shines out
karmic payback comes tenfold without a doubt.
To all you users and soul abusers who think you have a
beating heart..
see me from afar, I'm now a shooting star.
You get to go back and begin again at the start.

hope

Sinking still in my free will, I buy my time
while dying inside.
Tears they fall and drop alone
still nowhere to call my home.
Cast away for younger flowers
my body tires by the hour.
My HOPE is shadowed by darkness around
it's above and below without a sound.
It's passing in front and mocking me,
I project into a standing tree;
a standing tree that is so tall
umbrellas me as I feel small.
It's a reminder of seasons past
although it's now gloomy, this to shall pass.
Help me be as this tree, roots firmly planted
into the earth while reaching toward the sky.
It's never to long empty handed, neither am I.
.

voice

Turbulent soul runs away in haste
family forgotten remains in taste.
Another night another day
of wondering why my life is this way.
A visionary or a channeled being
I lay my head and aim for dreaming.
but…
Sleep escapes me.
I had a heart, house, and family
before I took this pen and was cursed by men.
I had a life of blinded faith, now it's different
questions still remain.
What is my purpose and what is my path?
How long can this misery last?
Misery loves company,
well it's been my company for years.
Pain washes through me in oceans of tears.
I stay to myself caught up in this waking dream.
My VOICE, sometimes a sexy whisper but deep inside a scream.
-I'm screaming for some sanity
-I'm screaming for resolution
Thank god I can put this music on cause rock and roll is never noise pollution
Thank god I can listen and lose myself in a verse,
of another's pain and another's curse.

I know I'm not alone in feeling this way.
-gotta get up now to face another day
-gotta go forward there is no going back
Sometimes walking, sometimes running, a full spirit I certainly don't lack.
A soul full of memories of hatred and love.
A life of puzzled tragedies were sent from above.
The more I write and the more I sing, sorrow built up leaves my twisted brain.
The more I live the more I feel, evolving into someone with strange appeal.
An anomaly of vision, speech and love,
an exaggerated mask fits like a tightly formed glove.
I'm going …
I'm going…
I'm going, again
I know
I really do know
Through thick and thin with all I am, it all comes back to where it began.

feeling

Death-
not of the body
of the soul
give up control
of the love
of the FEELING
of space
of emotion
of senses reeling
weightlessness
into being
of one with
the self
feels good
close your eyes
to feel
without seeing

giving

Once again my world is crumbling.
It never was built to last, filled with
unsteady hesitations, revisiting of the past.
Tear soaked hands once held by another
days pass and evolve...
another face, another lover.
Each moment presents itself.
I'm not ready for the lessons.
I'm tired in body, soul and mind,
and left with too many questions.
The world is spinning around me
shattered screams where I stand still.
Different players but same old game,
make me old and ill.
The only thing I'm good at is the GIVING of my soul.
Each day I gather parts of me, on a path to make me whole.

remembrance

All of them I shred with words, though it's a gift it's also a curse;
makes me so I can't sleep at night, blurs the lines of wrong and right.
Gives me memories I'd rather kill, and sweat filled dreams that make me ill.
The more I feel and the more I know it wears on me deep down in my soul.
Detached belief that all is alright, why does my body prepare to fight?
Wake up and fight to get through another day of wondering why my life is this way.
Happiness is a word that's foreign to me yet I am the only one capable to set my mind free.
There has to come a time when my questions are answered, when the puzzle in my head is no longer scattered.
There has to come a time when I wake up and feel useful.
I know I belong somewhere and to someone I matter.

Most days I'd rather silently exit.
Step back like I never ever existed
at all.
Walking this earth I feel like an alien with unblinking eyes.
I wait for the last fall although,
I have fallen many times.
This time...
my wings are shredded
body is bruised.
My mind is a constant whirlwind
its about all I can do to find a place that is quiet.
Try to be quiet while spirit comes in...
It's in those moments I remember
I do not walk alone.
I am reminded to see how much I've grown.
Sometimes even that knowledge
is fleeting, distant, and makes no sense.
If we really are spiritual beings having a human life
then I suppose all we do need is
REMEMBRANCE.

time

It's times like these
quick moments of peace
that make me believe
every place and every face
was part of the plan
a fate pre-decided
a charts flame was ignited
burned bright to light
the darkest hours
scrambled thoughts become clear
of every step guided here
to this place where my breath
rises and falls
mystery is still part of me
as always will be
TIME tells all

illusion

Take me back to the woods where most people are good
-help me rise up from the ashes I've seen
-help me through this life without becoming too mean
-help me I ask, so that I can help others
I thought that was my purpose, to be an eternal mother.
The way to this peace is by being a whore?
Who was I to believe, I could have been more.
Get up tomorrow, put on my best game face
believe to my bones there is a way out of this place.
A time when I will stand on that mountain so strong
a time when I'll feel like I finally belong.
Even if belonging means living in total seclusion…
the reality of life is, it's all an ILLUSION.

gently

In nature I see twos and pairs
one white bird shines she has no fear
standing tall on the bridge of life
she flies so proud
relieves her strife
glides so GENTLY through the trees
her spirit caught on a silent breeze

goddess

Do you believe in witches and warlocks?
Priests become preachers, women become Harlots.
Do you believe in those eyes of blue,
when they say they want to take care of you?
I hold to my beliefs even though you giggle.
The words I speak make you squirm and wiggle.
The rhymes I write seem like word play to you.
You don't even acknowledge its my goddess coming through.
My GODDESS, my god, don't want to share mine today.
Go ahead with your laughter, go find your own way.

becoming

Feel like I'm on a moving sidewalk,
standing still while others pass by.
I gaze outside the largest window,
and project myself into the sky.
BECOMING like a bird floating effortlessly in the wind.
Wings spread to capacity I fall and elevate again.
Effortless and weightless above the earth I feel.
Wings of an angel and butterfly, my energy no one steals.
Vibration matches magnetic wind
I catch my breath, elevate within.

truth

Sometimes in the stories of our mind
far from where our dreams do meet.
There's a place unknown where I need to go
you'll be waiting patiently.

Sometimes all you do is close your eyes
to find that place in life where dreams meet.
It's a lonely road, friends come and go
but I know you're waiting, for me.

Time is time and all we find
is our TRUTH from inside
it shines…
oh, it shines.

Time is time
all we are to find
is our truth from inside
let it shine, let it shine
from inside, let it shine.

accept

I've been fighting with my soul for how long I don't know.
I lay in my own fear, those I love are never near.
I wouldn't want them here to see me this way.
I often forget people don't think as I do.
Isolation and solitude sometimes give a better mood,
more often than not it keeps me down
believing that what goes, must also come around.
Got my blinders on for my goal straight ahead
no detours on the road this time.
To all you doubters and haters before
it's about to come out in simple rhyme.
Got a strength inside as I look in his eyes,
his words try to get me to reveal.
Little does he know who he's messing with,
there's nothing from me he will feel.
ACCEPT each day as it comes my way,
some are too much like the ones before.
Regardless of what you may see in me,
I'll always make a move toward the door.
If respect isn't given there's a better way of living
this I know for sure.

trying

My dreams, I don't remember them
but it seems I crush everyone else's dreams
with every day I live.
TRYING to be true to myself,
keep my thoughts boxed on the highest shelf.
Keep my heart tucked into a deep drawer
pulsing and bleeding, it's now crushed on a floor.
You say you hate me, how many times has that been said?
Hate on me with your face full of lies, yellow screen built
around your head
I do the best I can with every day I live.
I'm figuring out the best person I can be.
Always too much I seem to give, always too much pain and
guilt on me.

retreat

I listened to you speak
and now I sit with my tears.
Wish I could be calloused and jaded
then I'd match your lying vibration.
but,
The universe shows me all I need to see
in a matter of moments
you now mean nothing to me.
How quick life goes from sunshine to rain.
How quick the smile fades and the face shows new pain.
Why this life is so abrasive
I would really like to know.
It's like I've been black balled
from the feelings of joy.
Seems much easier to act like an immature boy
and walk around with not much
feelings of love or care;
to stop believing
there is a peaceful life somewhere.

-time to narrow my road stripe

-time to shrink my bubble

-time to box up my heart

...to keep me out of trouble

Time to be the observer and watch the wheel spin.

Time to caress and nurture myself

as I RETREAT

within.

someone

I was hoping I could see forever in your eyes.
At least you've been honest with me
no need for telling lies.
I really like the way I seemed to fit right in.
It was nice to try your world awhile
but now I must leave again.
I want to stay, not go away.
I want your love but thats for you to give.
I can't force you to be with me, to live.
There is someone else you remind me of
from so many years ago.
I wanted to stay with him to
but again I had to go.
How hard it is to find someone to love,
someone who loves me back.
SOMEONE who wants to share life with me
all the pleasures, pain and facts.
Share all the love the fears and joys,
all the insecurities from our inner girl and boy.

growing

With each rejection I know there is someone better for me.
Someone out there will eventually see what you don't see.
Someone who hasn't lost the feel of his own soul.
Someone who will look at me and see us both GROWING old.
I won't have to leave anymore, and he won't have to hide.
Together we will always be the Bonnie with the Clyde.
There's no such thing as growing old in our hearts.
We've come to know that laughter is truly the best medicine:
kisses are truly the best gift
time is non-existent
realities veil lifts
visually hot and magnetically bound
love is cyclical
our star is round
innocent eyes can see a truth
that is only found in the hearts of youth.

wonderment

Whatever happened to the Easy Bake oven,
making mud pies outside full of rocks, spit, and lovin'?
Whatever happened to late night hide-and-go seek,
sweat stained Saturday play clothes that proudly reeked;
Lite Brite, Payday, and Pick-Up Stix,
Tootsie Roll pops that questioned 'How many licks'?
PBS educational cartoons and Sesame Street,
Speed Racer in the morning and Soul-Train beats?
Whatever happened to Garanimals to,
when clothes were matched by animals found in a zoo?
Whatever happened to battery powered boom boxes blaring in the park,
where families and friends gathered and stayed way past dark?
Whatever happened to Fantasy Island and Love Boat,
and running around in the cold without a coat?
Whatever happened to sticking out your tongue at someone you didn't like
or showing up at a park with nothing but a kite?
Whatever happened to before bedtime tickle-fests?
You couldn't stop giggling when you were supposed to rest.

Its never to late to sometimes feel like a kid,
to go back and remember the things that you did;
to remember when the world was filled with WONDERMENT
and love,
to believe there was someone watching you from above.
Its never to late to go back to childhood
and now turn any bad stuff that happened into good.

poet

Your heart is not so rotten as to
make me forget about you.
If I placed a bracket around it
would that make it have more truth?
Fuck my mind but not my body
drink the essence of my soul.
Smile at me with that sideways glance I briefly came to know.
I always want what I can't have,
isn't that part of the human condition?
If I drove a Ferrari to visit you,
would that have granted me free admission?
I'm just a lonely POET stuck back
in a place called heartbreak hotel.
The strength in me is slowly showing
to get me through this emotional hell…

wish

I wished for you,
but I guess you didn't wish for me
have to remember
whatever will be, will be
time and time
I try to talk to you
but I'm often denied
what's a girl like me to do
so I just sit down and cry
I WISH you'd be the one
to say it's going to be ok
I wish you'd be the one
to mend my yesterday's
but I have to remember
whatever will be
will be

leeches

If there's ever a time when you feel like crying
you must stand strong while your heart is dying.
People all around are trying to bring you down.
I'm used to casting people aside, those that don't belong in my life.
I'm used to being used up, but now it's more like I'm fed up
with LEECHES, takers, and drama makers;
full of lust and greed take what you need,
all you have is all you see but you want more as you leech on me.
Leeches and creeps are the typical thieves
they don't take your money, they feed off your soul.
Take is all they do, take is all they know.

actions

When you say you will see me,
then don't even call
it makes me retreat because after all:
-I shouldn't be someone's option
-I shouldn't be someone's maybe
I should be someone's only one, they prefer to call 'baby'
A few nights ago there were tears in my eyes,
I was hoping time would show me you prioritized
a place for me and you to be
but…
As it's said, 'time tells all'
here this day, you didn't call.
Your ACTIONS tell me more than you could ever say.
I shouldn't have to feel this way.
Once again I will start to erase my dreams,
wishing you held a place in my heart.
I held out my hand where my heart did rest
but you handed it back, self proclaimed conquest.
Cycles repeat but not this time,
lesson is learned and spelled in rhyme.
Time to move on from what may have been,
you're not even close enough to call a friend.

blessings

A foolish heart got blown apart
by the breeze that blew today.
Should have known with the red flags thrown
this day would come my way.
A place in time makes one more rhyme
with many more to follow.
The calm in me has come to see
there is a better tomorrow.
Pain retains the souls complaint,
slowly light comes to surface.
One more time a sparkle shines
fruition of BLESSINGS remain un-purchased.
The numb and void my heart destroyed,
grows quiet far within;
and plants a seed someday I'll need
when love shall rise again.

anticipation

Master manipulators of the sickest kind,
see what they want and move in on your mind.
Smile on occasion and give you a laugh,
then begins the drain the leaves you aghast.
Mind fuck and thoughts twisted listening to every word you speak;
sorting through their grated brain then regurgitated with their tweaks.
It's not cause we're messed with as a child,
that makes us grow up misunderstood.
It's the leeches and vampires that drain our souls,
when you're in supposed adulthood.
With you I appeared weak but was waiting all along,
in quiet ANTICIPATION for the day I'd be gone.
Nobody takes my right to be me away, at least not for long.

release

Duality believe in me, conformity steals my mind.
I wonder when this joke is over, when you will see me and be kind.
Wonder when I'll rest my weary head,
instead of just wishing I'd be better off dead.
So much pain, anger and sorrow.
So much wishing for a better tomorrow.
How can you relate when you've not ever tasted my fear?
Never have been in my head, your cold heart won't come near.
I want to open up!
I want to love you!
but... you stand away
and let me be
alone.
You look at me as if you don't know me.
maybe you don't
maybe you won't
maybe I'm just usage like all the others
coming and going
useless wives, whores and mothers
What do you care?
You don't listen to me.
I thought you did, thought you were different
now I see...
There is nothing to RELEASE me
from you.

commitment

I am the one gliding and dipping into the depths of the seas
in earthly hell.
I am the one who has risen above where angels fly to
puncture an invisible veil.
I am the one committed in an imaginary insane asylum.
I am the one peaceful in present before becoming undone.
I am the one willing to stumble, crumble and fall
to keep rising again and again.
I am the one who if you tell me your heartache, I'll be your
most devoted friend.
I have no judgment if you're doing as you would want done
to you.
We are all partaking in this sometimes thoroughly messed up
human condition.
We're all seeking resolution from the pain life gives us.
Growth and awareness
COMMITMENT to ones path-
What you say and do as your truth
is the only fact that lasts.

pretend

What you need is redemption from yourself
because wherever you go you create a hell.
You suffocate spirits and pierce souls with words.
You sew them up in silence,
then PRETEND it's you who was hurt.
How can you play the victim
when you've mastered the mind fuck game?
It's hard to know your right from wrong
when you turn to others with blame.

boys

You are to me such an almost man,
haven't let go of mommies tit or her hand.
You keep on searching for that woman lost
destroying all at whatever cost.
Your simple weakness sickens me,
I'll soon be glad that I got free.
I should have known by the stories you told,
how this would end some day.
One minute I wish, I dream, you never came my way.
The last lesson in the chain of BOYS;
…you're not even worth being a boy toy, or worth the air I breathe.
So glad I woke up and made myself leave;
…you're nothing but pathetic inside and out, going nowhere without a doubt.

checkmate

I ain't got time for you play-uh
What was your name again?
Say it!
I don't remember half the shit you just said,
it went in one ear then straight out my head.
Your mouth is always running for the center of the show,
should maybe press the pause and rewind,
so you could possibly know.
Your head is so big it makes me wonder,
how you fit into a room.
Jeans so tight up on your ass,
I'm sure you'll be scratching soon.
talkity talkity talk talk talk...
Got a good game but don't got the walk.
Sometimes ya know a girl's got to sit back and wonder why,
I give someone like you the time in my life;
mostly out of amusement or something like that i think.
Oh shit! there goes your mouth again!
Hey bartender! Get me another drink!
Then, I'm 'bout to get up and leave this party behind.
Gonna spend my time finding a real man
who all he needs is to be kind;
with a fair amount of verbal exchange, a good heart, and
loving to.
oops, times up, games over
CHECKMATE
You and I are through.

found

I knew I would find you there
in a darkened corner somewhere.
In enough light for me to find
a mind as full and as weathered as mine.

What we've seen and where we've been
multi-dimensions swim within.
Unlock the part that held our hearts
echo's the beating of newly FOUND parts.

Rhythmic and melodic, tender and sweet
we found each other in time of need.
Warm and soothing, comfort and care
through birth of love we are aware.

planetary guidance
earthly resonance
solid formation
fluid & free
warm and tender
fiery & free

I see you
You see me

true

I'm unavailable for your call, because in my life after all...
A black heart casts a cloud of fear.
This rainbow shines you can't come near.
Got a prism of colors darkness can't touch.
Got a real love waiting that I've wanted so much.
Droplets dispersing the color around,
fall from this rainbow and kiss the ground.
They gently settle and reflect the sky.
Love does this magic, it makes me fly.
no more black clouds
no more black hearts
Love is within and around me.
TRUE love has its start.

birth

A veil of sludge has lifted.
Truth gave BIRTH through the dark night.
A hand falls limp unable to receive
a love that could set any wrong to right.
Claymation faces twist in surprise,
positive thoughts and dreams are not so wise.
Blackened heart, judgments cease
I find a way out, souls release.
Stepping softly into the morning light
the same ol' sun is there to greet me.
The same one seen many times before.
It rises to greet me with its welcoming rays,
promise of renewal, promise of a new day.

bond

The bluest eyes of a sunny sky,
his pores ooze of babies breath and sex.
I've wondered how he came my way,
and need him until my death.
A complexity of emotions and the simplicity combined
He,
knows exactly how to stimulate my mind.
Mortal time and physical pleasures,
each moment we have is like an unearthed treasure.
Although I know I must say goodbye,
for once in life I do not cry.
There seems to be an understanding
greater than known before;
whatever capacity this union brings
it's love that opened the door.
A knowing that is cellular recognition
each time I look into his eyes.
The sweetest face that can also send me into a headspace
questioning,
Why?
A prism of feelings we do exchange,
Wherever this life takes us the BOND of love remains.

formation

I looked into the sky last night and something caught my eyes.
It was glowing in the moonlight and made me wonder why…
Was it to soften my wounds and lift my heavy melancholy
or was it the Universe playing it's usual tricks on me?
What I saw was the perfect FORMATION of clouds shaped as a heart.
It quickly reminded me that is how true love starts;
not tossed about game playing through silence and fear
but openness and acceptance of long wasted years.
I'll just keep on waiting and watching the signs,
like that heart in the sky that caught my questioning eyes.
love is always within us and never without,
there is another soul waiting for me to bond together
without a doubt.

glance

There are moments in time frozen in my mind
a look into my eyes as we step apart.
Along separate ways we spend our days,
I sometimes feel you in my heart.
So much hurt and so much pain this life it gives and takes away.
Gives a GLANCE and quick memory
to tuck away on the days
I don't see you.
A poet is someone who observes then writes
of deepest emotions and turbulent plights;
of feelings shown then hidden away
to possibly surface another day.
There is a look, a knowing stare
and somehow I feel you are aware;
when we get our night to hang
the daylight comes and takes it away.
We each return to our separate lives.
How much is truth and how much lies?
Cycles of people come and go, live each day and let it show,
'Time tells all' I do believe.
From faith in the night's sky love was conceived.

angel

My voice has silenced except to those who will listen.
It's another situation, diamond in the rough starting to glisten.
An ANGEL holds the pencil with the eraser at one end,
erasing the dirty blotches soul light emerges from within.
A butterfly steps out of her cocoon.
A dormant flower begins to bloom.
A rainbow with a pot of gold at the end.
A bridge of love connected by friends.
A gentle breeze that stirs the stars.
My heart skips a beat whether you're near or far.
hearts and stars
stars and hearts
smiles and giggles
from the very start

smitten

I am SMITTEN so let it be written
for the past day and a half I've thought mostly of you.
Like a summer love slowly fading
the distance of your presence has created
a place in my mind reserved for you.
I wonder how many others you've affected this way
how many others have met you, then spent their days
with an affectionate longing,
a lip throbbing,
a heart beating,
for you.
I've always been a sucker for big beautiful blue eyes
yours are like no others, like a most perfect summer sky.
Your smile can be devilish, your laugh intoxicating,
your body a vision of art that keeps me contemplating;
When will I get to see you again?
When will I get to touch you again?
When will I get to place my two fingers on
each side of your spine and gently press
into your flesh so divine?
As I touched you once before on the dance floor
the darkened mark on your neck that says 'I am loved'
Yes, you are.

addicted

Make me be ADDICTED to you.
Fill me until the ache is gone.
Am I what you've waited for?
We've both wanted each other all along.
"Oh my god" he says.
This connection has nothing to do with a deity,
unless what we do brings out the best of you and me.
Wrap me in your strength.
Drench me in your sweat.
Pulsate until I no longer think
this moment I won't forget.
A satisfied yearning keeps me coming
back to you.
A release of this body like only you can do.
Primal beats of animalistic lust
coursing through the both of us.
Climactic closeness to the god of our seed
my head spinning, body quivering
it is you I need.

unopened

So many distorted days have come and gone,
the blanketed night turns to mornings fresh sun.
Some memories fade of a beautiful soul.
I still smell you, eyes of blue.
I see through you, trace the sway of your hips.
Imagine my touch upon the curve of your lips.
My heart aches for you, eyes of blue.
You're a treasure chest remained for me,
UNOPENED.
You said to write a song about you.
Would that bring you back to me again?
You're out there somewhere.
I feel you in my mind.
Amidst the drudgery of daily living,
your words were always kind.
I'm not sure you knew, how I felt about you.
I sat back and listened to your stories,
wishing I was in them, to breathe, to inhale your glory.
But…
you are gone,
I carry on.
I carry on.

expansion

Carnal pleasures of the flesh make me weak I must confess.
Candle flames illuminate the desires
of the soul that turn to hate.
Words are spoken, float above to thin air.
Eyes are in connection, we become aware.
This moment is only fleeting
head games are intact.
Role play is demeaning.
EXPANSION is a fact.
My third eye is growing tired of the scenarios I speak.
Yes, all this desire has come to make me weak
but…
I still want you.

memories

I immerse myself in a pool of warm blood
moonlight illuminates blue, skin surfacing is crimson red.
I step onto the unsteady stone.
My wet footprint lingers for a moment.
Only for a space in time, I open my minds eye
and find you're naked in it.
A breeze comes gently to stroke my skin
MEMORIES of you I keep within.
A loving touch, the sweetest kiss,
through the cycles of lifetimes
it's you that I've missed.

partner

I like the way this tear feels on my face
it reminds me to stay distant of this place.
It's all temporary this sadness I share.
I know there's a PARTNER waiting out there.
One who only wants company of the sweetest kind,
who wants to listen to the thoughts of my mind.
One who wants to walk and gently take my hand
who wants to smile and say "I'm your man".
Someone who will tell me the deepest of his dreams
and call me just to let me scream.
Someone not afraid to touch my face,
or say with a flirty voice "Hey, let's get out of this place"
…but
for now I feel this pain that reminds me I am alive.
I stare at the stars of this evenings lonely sky.
I continue to put one foot in front of the other
and keep walking my path alone;
for someone, someday that gives me
the feeling of, I am home.

mountain

There is a mountain that stands so very strong.
It is a place where I feel I sometimes belong.
A place where no one feeds me lies
its just me...
the earth and the sky.
I can gaze upon the traffic buzzing
so far from me below.
When I feel that life is crumbling,
it's to this mountain I go.
A birds eye view of life passing by,
a place where I used to sit and cry.
This mountain makes me stand tall and strong,
it absorbs my grief and pain.
When my time on this great earth has passed,
this MOUNTAIN will remain...
The clouds in the sky have parted, sunlight came shining through.
A suns ray landed on my shoulder,
as if to say 'I will comfort you.'
'I am here to lift you when this life is hurting too much,
remember to come to this mountain side
and feel its loving touch.'
'Remember to sit and be awhile, remember that you are loved.
When you feel this life is getting to you,
know there is someone for you above
...my love.'

stillness

We get caught up in the troubles of our mind,
searching for a place where spirit can unwind.
A flicker of light as a firefly are we... passing by;
as small as it's light in the vast night sky.
Our inner turmoil disappears.
While immersed in nature, inner truth is near.
Each step taken walks us farther from the past.
Each breath taken brings us into this exact moment known.
STILLNESS in stone, molecular memory calls us home.

awakened

This life has made me well aware
of what a girl like me has to give and care.
It's made me turn a calloused eye
at the profound tragedies that have gone by.
It's given me a taste of freedom
and then reminded me of who really won.
It's tormented me and crushed my shadow.
It's made me believe in no better tomorrow.
It's given me temptation overload,
only to sit back from view and gloat.
Suspended sensuality of all that has yet to be.
Liquid ecstasy of all that can be,
consumes the cells of all that see me.
AWAKENED and alive will always be me.
I am free.

...afterthought

each of us have our own
stories to tell
our own structures and layers
of personal hell
our own joys, sorrows, and
goals for tomorrow
may you understand these poems
are but a layer, a rhyme
words and feelings gathered
from a small space in time

www.ingramcontent.com/pod-product-compliance
Lightning Source LLC
Chambersburg PA
CBHW052028290426
44112CB00014B/2426